Mnemosyne: A Reservoir

Ashley Abigail Resurreccion

BookLeaf
Publishing

India | USA | UK

Presentation by *BookLeaf Publishing*

Web: www.bookleafpub.com

E-mail: info@bookleafpub.com

ISBN: 9789358737004

First edition 2023

Mirror

Your silhouette is balanced with paper cuts,
Black and white
Like the edges that surround you

In these spaces, I see tears
Bold colors
Heavy burdens

Histories blending in the background
Shape the foreground of your portrait

To Explore A Mood

A disquieting mood
Thunders into the foreground

With and without you
I stand still yet feel unsettled
By the dangers of loss
And celebrations of growth

We're told life's path is fairly linear
Go to work, find a partner, make a home
Supposedly everything has its place
A perceived safety guide for time
Society suggests you to follow

No one talks about alternatives
Or the opportunities you'll find
Way away from the anchors of 'here'

Because when you wander alone
There are no blueprints

One Moment

The discord between my
Thoughts and emotions
Strangled me
Amplified my awareness
Or perhaps dulled it
So I can't feel anything
Yet I told myself

Keep going
Keep going
Keep going,

Because
I spent my whole life
Waiting for this moment
And when it came
It was too late to realize
I never needed it at all

Decades of Absence

It took me 20 years to figure out
These decades of your absence
Filled me with dread
Drained me of intimacy
And burst volatile emotions
When I least expected them to

To learn neglect aversion and silence
are all forms of communication
Not moments to wait
For love and care
To be reciprocated

I learned to adjust my life
To your absence
To fear those who promised safety
Instead of embracing those
Who freely, truly choose
To accept me as I am

So when you came into my life
Without warning
Expecting me to be
Someone looking up to you or
Dropping unshared expectations or

Unwilling to create friction in the shadows

I may have cried or
Stuttered from the shock or
Felt shaken
The same way I did when you first left,

But I knew better and collected myself
Since it's over now
I can decide to let go
And declare
I never needed you at all

A Glimpse of Grief

When love has no destination
I wonder if I did all the right things
And why I still feel so wrong

Between needs and wants,
Perceived comforts of familiarity
Blanket internalized insecurities
You are long gone

It is part of my normal
To think of the wrappers from your cigarettes
Bags from food we shared
Or equally discarded materials
Easily and immediately lost
Faded memories after the moments are gone

Grief comes in cycles yet
My feelings cast a silver lining too
Impromptu smiles amidst the cries I make
Whenever I think of you

This Is Lacuna

Energy comes and goes
As I learn how to make it so
The material feels consistent and
I feel confident with how things stand
And I spend countless hours practicing
But the stresses are exhausting

Extending beyond the physical form
To people and places that surround me
Molding my thoughts deeply
My actions crumble
Like clay when it gets dry
With too many impressions
And not enough water

I'm trying my best
To do something good but
I need to take a break
Because I'm failing

I don't want to do this any more
Create art in anger to hide my shame

So I recite to myself gently
I don't blame you for
Finding solace in self-sabotage

I Found My Voice

I struggled to express
Focusing on healing
Every part of me at once
Isn't simple

Until I had the courage to change
Share that I cannot give
Take time for myself
and come home
Without diminishing connection

So I remind myself to
Please be tender
Wherever you go
Find your rhythm
Build your own shelter

Consciously noticing
Embracing new habits and feelings
Will help you love yourself
For who you truly are

Give yourself a session to meditate
To voice 'no' to the gravity of negativity
Because your body is its own sanctuary

Why do so much to take care of others
When there's no one to take care of you?

Special

Key moments can represent
Triumph
Failure
Or any emotion
About how things got to this point
But if the moment is something
That lingers
Maybe it's worth exploring
Regardless of whether it becomes
Part of the chronology of
Our life
Our love
Our future
Or the attention we give
To transform one another now

First Try

Time and certainty
Would help you understand
I feel so much more
Secure
So much
Stronger
Able to give
All that you need
When we are ready
But we cannot move
Unless we are both
In opposite directions
Willing to
Try First

To See the Consequence

The consequence of being prematurely
Honest with you
Left us alone together

Yet we had no shame
In any feelings which made us
Uncomfortable
Or potential promises
Which cannot at any required moment
Be commanded
Withdrawn and
Respected

Whether we chase pleasure without purpose
Or find meaning in life beyond present moments
Only we can reify states of pure abundance

To Relapse

Why should I work so hard
To calm anxiety
About our distance

I will (not) repeat
Mistakes from before
We're always in
The figuring it out phase

Not knowing
Where either of us
Will end up
We can be happier

Within a universe full of strangers
Watching the stars,
Playing games,
Constantly in motion

Indulging in a simple phone call
A stream of tears or yells or laughter
Can lead all of us to an ocean
Of forgiveness and joy

Liminal time and space

Is meant to be spent in new ways
So we can see beyond the horizon

To Be Vulnerable

Her own cares
And not his
Were troubling her
It was natural that he fully sympathized

Imagine the relief
Embracing each other in this sanctuary
He stood silent and smiled
As she gazed up into his face

And then, kissing her forehead
The floodgates were opened
She could not help responding with a smile
To the love in his eyes

Did I Find Paradise?

What have I done?
I had done nothing at all

I don't care for ignorance
Embarrassment
Indignation
Or contempt
The excuses you tell me through tears

But if you really wish to know existence
We can love

Purely
Passionately
Plainly

To have Paradise in the mundane and novel
There is no pressure to perform with you
This genuine radiance reminds me of home

I Found Release

Have a good time
And no expectations

Our love, if it could grow stronger
Would do so because
After all that has happened
We are still venturing together

Separately or not
Through curiosity and shared consciousness
There is no happiness comparable
To being in community

Everyone has their flaws and falls
What matters is
How we respond to them
And own ours

Because when one asks "Do you love me?"
And the other replies, "Yes"
This filter for disillusionment
Renders me humble enough

To know that I'm replaceable
Yet you're still here

In the Frames

When I learn how to frame this
And look through others' lenses
Maybe it could change
How I move forward

So I buy new frames
Small with tinted lenses
And bright plastic
Because I don't need gold

Knowing I have pyrite
Reassures me that there's value
In knowing how to get anywhere
Or do anything
With the little I have

For now I can keep changing
Until I won't need to know everything
In the frames

I Made Progress

Some of the dreams that guide us
Are the same dreams that bind us
But who am I
To question the pulse
Of timeless advance
Or forces of nature
Steps towards progress
That make us who we are

Sewing Sutures

I am finally ready
To sew the sutures
Where I cut my heart out
On a canvas
And braided tears for my eyes
I pulled them out
With great relief
Though the scars stay
There is no deadline
For healing

The Final Spark

I was struggling with reality
Bargaining time to avoid my own
Any time I felt disconnected

By developing the capacity
To be imperturbable
I realized I didn't need
To control anything that disturbs me

So I burned my old art into Ash
To spark a Resurreccion
And be myself

I admit I picked up
The remains that survived
Yet this process
No longer meant I was weak
Had a scarcity mindset
Or was missing something
As if I was never whole

Peace came
From cherishing myself
In ways others never will
And I cannot imagine a future

Without the love that exists
From being at home
Within my own soul